CCSS **Genre** Realistic Fi

**Essential Question**
**How do writers look at success in different ways?**

MW00736511

# THE FINAL

by Paul Mason
illustrated by S G Brooks

# Chapter 1
# A NEW FORWARD

Only five minutes remained of the game—five short minutes between making the dizzying heights of the finals tournament or finishing another season with a whimper. The score was tied at 1-1.

Elisa, watching her team from the bench, could hardly breathe. She couldn't bear to watch the Pumas lose, even though she hadn't had much of a chance to come off the bench and play this season.

Just then, a defender slammed into the back of Tia, the Pumas' forward, who had the ball at her feet. The referee blasted his whistle and called foul. He gave a free kick to the Pumas—it would probably be the last kick of the game.

Jenny lined up to take it, then ran forward, kicking the ball high toward the goal, hoping someone would rise up to meet it. Sure enough, there was Tia. A massive leap, head and shoulders above the others, almost as if she were hovering in midair.

*Thump!* Tia connected, sending a header blasting past the goalkeeper into the back of the net. Tia hit the ground, her body rolling awkwardly as the final whistle blew.

The crowd went wild, no one noticing until the excitement had died down that Tia was still lying on the ground.

Coach Lee ran onto the field, quickly realizing that Tia was injured. She shouted to Tia's dad for some ice.

The Pumas' jubilation became muted as they watched their star player lying on the grass with ice on her ankle.

Elisa kneeled beside her and touched her teammate's shoulder. "How does it feel?" she asked anxiously.

"I'll be okay," Tia replied, smiling with clenched teeth.

The next day at practice, though, it was clear that things weren't going to be okay at all. The sight of Tia hobbling on crutches, her leg in a cast, told the team that there was no way she was going to play in the finals tournament.

Coach Lee called the team together. "Now, you've probably guessed that with Tia injured, I'll be looking for a new forward."

As the team ran onto the field, Elisa approached Tia. "I'm really sorry you can't play," she said.

"I still can't believe it, but thanks," Tia replied, shrugging. "Are you going to try for my position?"

Elisa nodded. "I want to."

At home, Elisa rushed to tell her brother Raul the news. The forward's role was dangling in front of her like a giant carrot, and she was going to do whatever was needed to grab the opportunity.

"You're definitely good enough," Raul said. "You've just got to push yourself to do it."

"Yeah, I figured you'd say that."

"I'll tell you one thing, though—the finals tournament is a whole different ball game. The best teams in the district will be there. You'll need to be ready."

# Chapter 2

# REALITY CHECK

That weekend, the Pumas and their families headed to the park for a barbecue to celebrate making the finals.

While the parents were getting the food ready, Becky, the Pumas' captain, noticed a group of girls on the soccer field. "Hey, let's challenge them to a game," she said.

Elisa followed her gaze. The girls looked like they were the same age as them. "I bet we can beat them," Jenny said, and she ran up to the girls. Elisa and the others followed.

"You don't have long," Jenny's dad called. "Lunch will be ready soon."

Becky introduced herself to one of the girls and asked if they wanted to play. The girls agreed. "You want to mix up the teams?" one girl asked.

"No," Becky said. "If it's okay with you, we'll stick with our team." She grinned as she ran down the field to her position in goal.

Elisa got ready for the kickoff. Then she rolled the ball back to Jenny. Game on!

In a flash, a girl from the other team was in front of Jenny. She barely had time to pass the ball to Sarah. Sarah surged forward with the ball at her feet, looking to make a cross pass. Elisa ran down the center to meet it, but it never arrived.

Sarah was tackled, and four quick passes later, Becky was fishing the ball out of the back of the net. The other team had scored against them.

By the time the Pumas were rescued by the call to lunch, the score had ballooned to 6–1, and the other team hadn't even broken a sweat. "Great game," one of them said, laughing, as Elisa and the others slunk away. Elisa could only shake her head—she was out of practice, and it showed.

"I just hope we don't have to face those girls in the tournament," Becky said.

"Maybe all the other teams will be as good as that," Elisa pointed out. "We'll just have to step it up a notch." The other girls said nothing, but they looked dejected as they made their way back to their families.

At the next practice, the girls talked about the pick-up game in the park.

"The ball was glued to their feet," Jenny said.

"And they were fast," Becky added.

"Well, those are two things that you can work on," Coach said, pointing at the field. "I want line sprints. You know the routine!"

After 20 minutes of sprinting, the girls' faces were glowing. "My legs are shaking," grumbled Sarah.

"You're not done yet," Coach Lee said with a wicked smile. "Now, dribble around each cone, then take a shot at the goal before Becky can close you down. Let's go!"

Elisa raced to the front of the line, eager to be the first. She felt good with the ball at her feet—in control. She guided the ball around the cones, swapping neatly from right foot to left, before firing at the goal. Becky leaped at full stretch and just managed to push the ball wide.

"You're going to have to try harder than that," she said with a smile.

"I plan to," Elisa answered, sprinting to the back of the line to wait her turn again.

# Chapter 3

# DETERMINATION

At the end of the week, Coach Lee arranged a practice game and gave Elisa her first start. Though the Pumas just managed to scrape out a draw and were lucky to do that well, it was clear that Elisa was the most determined player on the field.

"We could have done better," Elisa said afterward to Coach Lee while zipping up her tracksuit.

"You did well, Elisa. Keep it up," Coach Lee said. She could see how much Elisa wanted Tia's position— there was a buzz around her, and the others were picking up on it.

"How'd the game go?" Raul asked when Elisa got home.

"Pretty good," said Elisa. "I scored a goal, but the other team was stronger. Do you have time to do a few drills before dinner?"

Out in the yard, Elisa and Raul passed the ball back and forth like a yo-yo. Then Raul made Elisa dribble the ball around the yard until it was too dark to see.

After what seemed like endless practice games, passing routines, and line sprints, Coach Lee announced the tournament team at the Pumas' final practice. "Becky, you're in goal. Jenny and Sarah, I want you both midfield."

Elisa's stomach churned as Coach read out the other names. "Let it be me, after all that extra work in the yard with Raul. Let it be me!" she thought.

Coach turned to Elisa. "And as forward, I'm going with Elisa, who's managed to attain new levels of consistency in training."

Elisa let out a sigh as the rest of the team clapped, and at practice that day, she pushed herself harder than ever.

On the day of the tournament, Elisa felt an extra jolt of energy running through her body as she pulled on her Puma shirt. This was it.

She and the other players tried to stay focused as they listened to Coach's final instructions.

As they went out on the field, Elisa took a look around. The Pumas were playing in front of a much bigger crowd than they were used to.

Elisa ran to the center to wait for the whistle. She smiled at the opposing player, but the girl didn't smile back. The girl wasn't smiling at the end of the game either, as her team slunk away after losing the game by two goals.

Elisa noticed Raul and her parents in the crowd and waved to them. Her brother ran over. "That was some goal to open the scoring," he said, beaming.

"Thanks," Elisa said. "Let's just hope we can keep the pressure on."

The semifinal was a lot tougher, though, and if Becky hadn't pulled off some great saves, the Pumas could have been four goals down by halftime.

At the start of the second half, things began to improve. Elisa passed across the field to Jenny, and her friend smashed it right into the goal. They were leading!

Then the other team went on the attack, and for the rest of the game, the Pumas found themselves defending hard to hold on to their lead. At last, the referee blew the whistle, and against the odds, they were through to the final.

"That was some performance! You kept us in the game," Coach Lee said, patting Becky on the back. "Now we have a chance to rest before the final. It's against the Cobras, last year's winners, and you're going to need everything you've got."

Elisa looked over at the team on the other side of the field, who had "Cobras" written on their orange shirts. "Look who it is," she said, pointing.

Sarah screwed up her face. "It's the girls from the park."

"They'd better not think they're getting six goals past us this time," Elisa said.

# Chapter 4
# THE COBRAS BITE

The Cobras kicked off the final, passing the ball around neatly, finding each other with ease. Elisa and the others fought hard but struggled to get possession of the ball. It was as if they were chasing shadows, just like that day at the park.

Again and again, the Pumas were pushed up to their goal line, defending fiercely all the way. Not once but twice, Sarah managed to just clear the ball as it sped toward the net.

Jenny threw herself into every tackle as she fought to prevent the Cobra forward from taking shots at the goal, while Becky dived left and right to keep the ball out of the net. The Pumas were in trouble, and they knew it.

Then just before halftime, Elisa timed a tackle to perfection, stealing the ball from an opposing player and bolting down the field before the Cobras could react. There was no one in front of her except the goalkeeper.

With the goal in sight, Elisa held on to her nerve, took her time, and struck the ball sweetly. The Cobras' keeper dived to the left, gloved hand outstretched as the ball flew past her into the net. GOAL!

The Puma supporters roared their approval, Raul louder than all the rest. None of them could believe the Pumas had taken the lead.

But if Elisa and their fans thought it was too good to be true, it was. Elisa's goal just made the Cobras lift their game a notch and then another. The Pumas were back to chasing shadows.

Five minutes to go, and the Pumas were down 3–1. The Cobras were in possession and had no intention of giving up the ball, passing it around easily. It was clear now that they were the better team.

When the referee blew the final whistle, Elisa and the others shook hands with the Cobras and sank to the grass, exhausted.

Coach Lee had a big smile on her face. "Great game, girls! Well done."

"You're not upset?" Jenny asked, gasping for breath.

Coach was surprised. "Upset? Why would I be upset? You girls fought your way into the final and played your hearts out right to the end. That's a triumph in any book. You were great!"

The team looked at each other and smiled. Coach was right—even though they'd lost, they had played as hard as they could, and you couldn't take that away from them.

The forward from the Cobras broke away from her team's celebrations and came over. "That's the hardest game we've played yet—that was some goal you scored," she said, nodding to Elisa.

"Thanks. You were just too good for us," Elisa said, getting to her feet. "Might not be the same story next time," she added with a grin.

The girl laughed. "I'll look forward to it. See you around," she said and went over to rejoin her team.

"The tournament's not for another year," Elisa said to Becky. "There's plenty of time to get in some practice drills. Shall we meet in the park tomorrow?"

Becky smiled and gave her friend a high five. "You took the words right out of my mouth."

# Summarize

Use the most important details from
*The Final* to summarize the story.
Your graphic organizer may help.

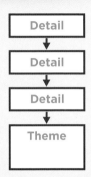

# Text Evidence

**1.** What features of the story help you identify it as
realistic fiction? **GENRE**

**2.** What is the theme of this story? How does Elisa's
achievement in Chapter 3 help you figure out
the theme? **THEME**

**3.** What does *slunk away* on page 6 mean? What is
the author trying to show? **CONNOTATION AND
DENOTATION**

**4.** Write about how Elisa becomes successful at soccer.
Use details from the story in your answer.
**WRITE ABOUT READING**

**Compare Texts**

Read about a person who is waiting to perform in a talent show.

# Talent Show

The school hall was about to burst,

Fourth Grade Idol being the cause.

Sadie so wanted to go on first

And bask in roaring applause.


Like a mouse she peeked from backstage

As Violet played tuba—no flaws.

When was her turn? It felt like an age

Waiting to bask in loud applause.

17

Next came Jada the sly magician,

Then Sam's parrots who talked without pause,

Putting dents in Sadie's ambition

To bask in polite applause.


Sunshine Nancy danced her ballet,

Stand-up Jack scored loud guffaws,

Now Sadie's nerves began to fray,

Scared there'd be little applause.


"No time to be nervous," Miss Ramos called out.

"No excuses, no grasping at straws."

Pale Sadie was wracked with doubt—

Would they give her any applause?


Sadie sang a soft birdlike tune,

A sweet song as frail as gauze.

Any moment she felt she'd swoon,

Certain there'd be no applause.

But as she warbled, the audience warmed,

The sweet melody made their hearts thaw.

And in the end, to their feet they stormed

And gave her worthy applause.

Now, bright Sadie,
she did not win.

The gold went to
Sam and his macaws,

But the proud singer
just said with a grin,

"Who cares? I sang
out of my skin,

And as long as I live, I will never begin

To forget that roaring applause."

## Make Connections

How does the writer help you to understand how Sadie feels about the result of the talent show?
ESSENTIAL QUESTION

How do Elisa in *The Final* and Sadie in "Talent Show" achieve their goals? TEXT TO TEXT

# Focus on Literary Elements

**Repetition** Poets use repetition to help their readers understand a message. Repeating a word or a phrase makes readers slow down and take notice. This encourages them to focus on the meaning of the words. Repetition also helps a poem achieve a rhythm that matches the meaning of the words, actions, or feelings the poem is expressing.

**Read and Find** In "Talent Show," the repetition of the last lines of every verse helps us understand how important the applause is to Sadie, and her anxiety about how much applause she will get when she performs. When the poem is read aloud, the rhythm of the last line and the small but important changes help to show Sadie's increasing anxiety. In the final verse, the repeated line shows that Sadie feels satisfied with her achievement.

## Your Turn

Work with a group to create a multimedia version of the poem. Read the poem aloud several times until you can feel the rhythm and your voice follows Sadie's feelings. Make an audio recording of your reading. Create a soundtrack, series of drawings, or a set of physical movements to accompany the recording. Share your work with the class.